NATIONAL
MONUMENTS
of the
U.S.A.
Activity Book

WIDE EYED EDITIONS

WELCOME TO THE NATIONAL MONUMENTS OF THE U.S.A.!

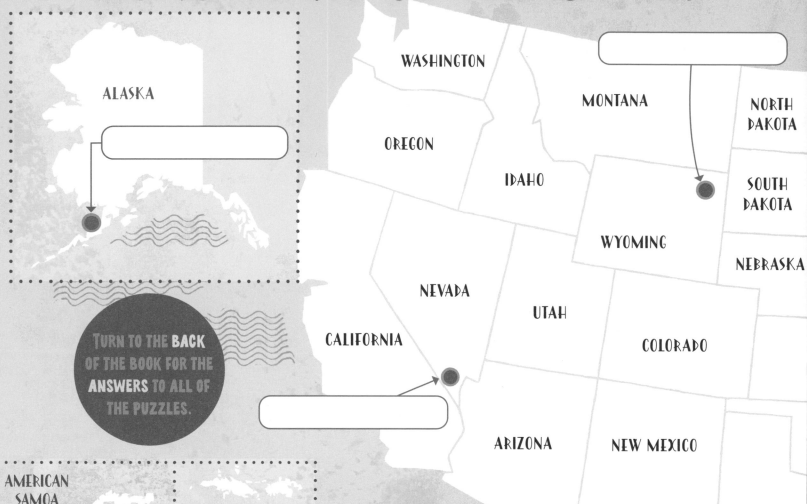

ALASKA

WASHINGTON

MONTANA

NORTH DAKOTA

OREGON

IDAHO

SOUTH DAKOTA

WYOMING

NEBRASKA

NEVADA

UTAH

CALIFORNIA

COLORADO

ARIZONA

NEW MEXICO

TEXAS

TURN TO THE **BACK** OF THE BOOK FOR THE **ANSWERS** TO ALL OF THE PUZZLES.

AMERICAN SAMOA

VIRGIN ISLANDS

HAWAII

DID YOU KNOW?
Today, there are around 130 national monuments. They are protected because they are historically, culturally, or scientifically important.

DEVILS TOWER
The first-ever national monument was created in 1906.

MINGYOW

PAPAHĀNAUMOKUĀKEA
This monument is the largest of them all. It's bigger than all the U.S. national parks put together!

WAIHIA

STATUE OF LIBERTY
This is one of the most visited monuments – and the most famous! It's shared between two states.

ENW OKRY

WEN SEYREJ

2

You are about to take a trip around the amazing national monuments of the U.S.A. As you complete the activities in this book, you'll discover historic places, extraordinary landscapes, special plants, and awesome animals.

Let's get started!

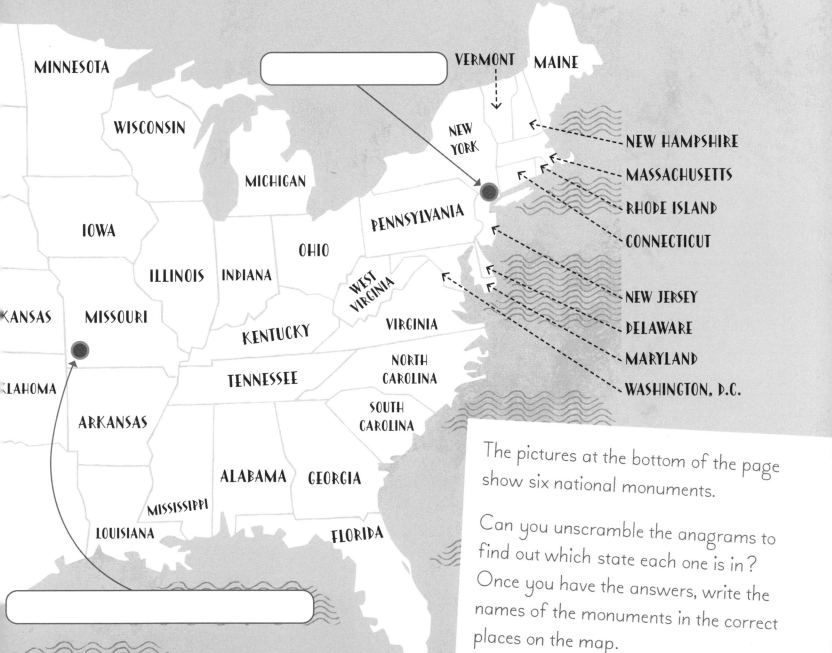

The pictures at the bottom of the page show six national monuments.

Can you unscramble the anagrams to find out which state each one is in? Once you have the answers, write the names of the monuments in the correct places on the map.

ANIAKCHAK

This is one of the least visited monuments. Only a few hundred people travel here each year.

SAKALA

☐ ☐ ☐ ☐ ☐

AVI KWA AME

Established in 2023, this is one of the newest monuments. The land it protects is considered sacred by the Mojave and other Indigenous peoples.

VADANE

☐ ☐ ☐ ☐ ☐ ☐

GEORGE WASHINGTON CARVER

This monument was the first to be dedicated to a non-president and to an African American. It is the birthplace of a renowned scientist.

SOURSIMI

☐ ☐ ☐ ☐ ☐ ☐ ☐ ☐

Statue of Liberty in Numbers

Since 1886, Lady Liberty has greeted immigrants and travelers alike—and for many, she symbolizes the freedom and equality that people hope to find in the U.S. How much do you know about this famous national monument?

Draw lines to match each of the descriptions on this page to the correct number. One has been completed for you.

Number of days it took for the statue to cross the ocean from France, the country where it was made. It was a gift of friendship to the United States.

Number of rays in the statue's crown (count them!).

27

2

100

12 million

377

7

8

Number of steps visitors have to climb to reach the crown.
HINT: The statue is the height of a 22-story building.

The number of people who arrived in the U.S. through Ellis Island between 1892 and 1954. People think about 40 percent of Americans have at least one ancestor who came to Ellis Island.

Length of the statue's index finger, in feet.

HINT: this picture shows roughly how big the finger is compared to a 5-foot-tall person.

The statue's copper sheeting is just $\frac{3}{32}$ of an inch thick. This is the thickness of how many pennies placed together?

In the 1980s, the Statue of Liberty had a major restoration for her centennial celebration. How many years old was she on this big birthday?

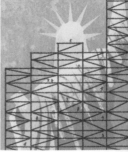

How Big?!

Lady Liberty's feet are big—very big!

Using the information below, can you work out the three-digit shoe size that rangers have estimated she would need to take?

271 None of these numbers are correct

715 One of these numbers is correct but in the wrong place

629 Two of these numbers are correct and in the right place

The Statue of Liberty's feet are stepping over a broken shackle and chain, a symbol of the end of slavery in the U.S.

STUDY THE SCENE

Study the picture below for 30 seconds.
Then turn the page and answer the questions about the scene.

Write your answers to the "Study the Scene" memory challenge here.

1. HOW MANY SAILBOATS ARE THERE IN THE SCENE?

2. WHAT IS THE GIRL HOLDING?

3. WHAT TYPE OF AIRCRAFT IS IN THE SKY?

4. WHICH ARM IS THE STATUE OF LIBERTY HOLDING UP THE TORCH WITH — LEFT OR RIGHT?

5. WHAT ANIMAL IS SHOWN IN THE SCENE?

6. HOW MANY FLAGS ARE THERE IN THE PICTURE?

WELCOME TO THE U.S.A.!

If you were designing a statue to welcome new arrivals to the U.S.A.. what would it look like? Draw your design on this empty plinth.

March for Equality

Some national monuments tell the stories of buildings or neighborhoods that have helped this country become a more equal place for everyone. Three of these important monuments are pictured below.

Can you help this group of marchers find a route that takes them past all three national monuments? They are only allowed to use each path once and must not retrace their steps.

START HERE

STONEWALL NATIONAL MONUMENT,
New York
Commemorates an uprising in 1969 that was an important turning point in the movement for LGBTQ+ rights.

BELMONT-PAUL WOMEN'S EQUALITY NATIONAL MONUMENT,
Washington D.C.
Celebrates the women who protested, marched, and were arrested as they worked for suffrage, the right to vote.

BIRMINGHAM CIVIL RIGHTS NATIONAL MONUMENT,
Alabama
Commemorates people, places, and events that were critical to the civil rights movement.

THE END

Amazing Animals

All kinds of awesome animals make their homes in the national monuments.

Take a look at the picture clues below, then fill in the crossword grid opposite with the names of the animals. You can look at the word bank if you need help.

ACROSS

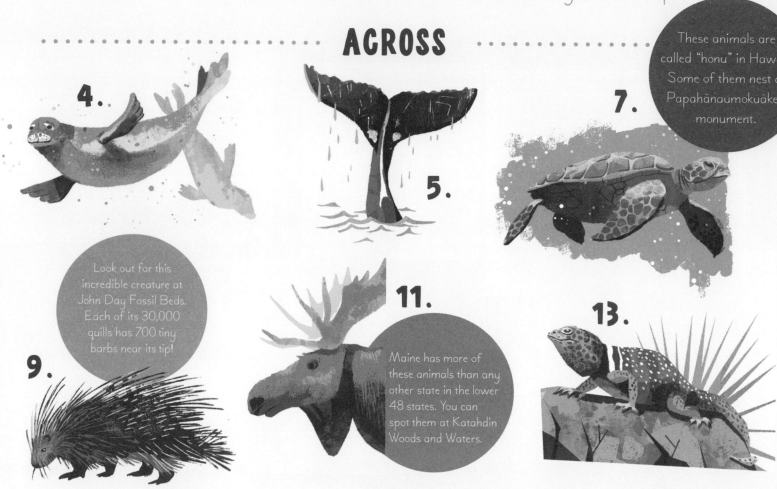

These animals are called "honu" in Hawaii. Some of them nest at Papahānaumokuākea monument.

4.

5.

7.

Look out for this incredible creature at John Day Fossil Beds. Each of its 30,000 quills has 700 tiny barbs near its tip!

9.

11.

Maine has more of these animals than any other state in the lower 48 states. You can spot them at Katahdin Woods and Waters.

13.

DOWN

1.

2.

3.

4.

6.

These animals live along the Alaska coast, including at Aniakchak monument. Sometimes they sleep holding hands so they don't drift away from each other.

8.

10.

12.

WORD BANK

BEAR	LIZARD	SEAL	WHALE
FOX	MOOSE	SQUIRREL	WOLF
JACKRABBIT	PORCUPINE	TOAD	
JELLYFISH	SEA OTTER	TURTLE	

At Craters of the Moon and other monuments, you might spot the fastest land animal in the United States. It can run at 60 miles per hour, and could even beat a cheetah in a long-distance race!

To reveal its name, use the letters on the yellow squares to fill in the missing letters in the word below.

P _ O _ G O _ N

THE FIRST AMERICANS

Some national monuments protect the culture and tell the stories of Indigenous peoples, including Native Alaskans, Native Americans, and Native Hawaiians. Many of these places remain sacred to Indigenous people today.

In the table below, each letter is represented by a number.
First, fill in all of the missing numbers, then use the table to de-code the names of six monuments that protect sites important to America's Indigenous people.
Finally, draw lines to match each monument to the correct picture and description.

A	B	C	D	E	F	G	H	I	J	K	L	M	N	O	P	Q	R	S	T	U	V	W	X	Y	Z
1		3			6					11				16							23				26

16 9 16 5 19 20 15 14 5

_ _ _ _ _ _ _ _ _

ALASKA

The Indigenous Tlingit people helped to establish this island monument in 1978. They call it Kootznoowoo, meaning "fortress of the bear."

UTAH

One of the world's largest natural bridges, this site is held sacred by several Indigenous nations, including the Navajo.

13 15 14 20 5 26 21 13 1   3 1 19 20 12 5

18   1   9   14   2   15   23   2   18   9   4   7   5

--- --- --- --- --- --- --- --- --- --- --- --- ---

WYOMING

This volcanic pillar is a sacred place for more than 26 Indigenous nations. It got its devilish name from a mistranslation.

ARIZONA

The Sinagua people began carving this extraordinary "castle" out of the cliff around 900 years ago.

1   4   13   9   18   1   12   20   25   9   19   12   1   14   4

4   5   22   9   12   19   20   15   23   5   18

--- --- --- --- --- --- --- --- --- --- ---

HAWAII

This 1,350-mile-long chain of ancient islands includes many sites sacred to Native Hawaiians.

MINNESOTA

The soft red stone of the quarries here has been used by the Dakota, the Lakota, and other Indigenous people to make sacred pipes for thousands of years.

16   1   16   1   8   1   14   1   21   13   15   11   21   1   11   5   1

--- --- --- --- --- --- --- --- --- --- --- --- --- --- --- --- ---

THRILL-SEEKERS

Hiking, canoeing, snow-shoeing, rock climbing, scuba-diving . . . there are lots of adventurous ways to explore the national monuments!

Below are three people, three outdoor activities, and three monuments. Using the clues at the bottom of the page, can you work out who visited which monument, and what they did there? As you discover the answers, fill in the grid next to the clues.

ADAM

CROSS-COUNTRY SKIING

MISTY FJORDS, ALASKA

This glacier-carved wilderness is part of the largest intact coastal rainforest in the U.S.

LAILA

WHITEWATER RAFTING

KATAHDIN WOODS AND WATERS, MAINE

This national monument protects 87,500 acres of mountains, woods, and tumbling rivers.

OMAR

SEA KAYAKING

DINOSAUR, COLORADO AND UTAH

Some people call this monument one of the quietest places in the West! It covers more than 210,000 acres of wilderness in two states.

CLUES

1. Omar did not get into a boat.

2. The person who went rafting visited a state next door to Wyoming. (Use the map at the front of the book to help you.)

3. Neither Adam nor Omar went to Misty Fjords.

NAME	ACTIVITY	NATIONAL MONUMENT

SMALL AND BEAUTIFUL

At the national monuments, you'll find huge caves, giant trees, massive mountains, and towering monuments. But look closely, and you'll see many tiny wonders too!

In this grid, fill in each square with one of these cute creepy-crawlies. You can draw them or write their name.

BEE
Grand Staircase-Escalante in Utah is buzzing with at least 660 different bee species. Some are tiny, while others are as big as your thumb.

BUTTERFLY
At Pipestone monument, Minnesota, migrating monarch butterflies arrive in late spring to feed on milkweed.

STINK BEETLE
What's that smell? These stinky beetles are found at Bandelier, in New Mexico. They squirt out a smelly liquid to protect themselves from predators.

BANANA SLUG
Big, yellow, and slimy, these eye-catching slugs are found at Muir Woods in California.

Each row, column, and mini 4 x 4 grid must contain all four animals.

Bird Search

Some national monuments are important stops on a migratory bird flyway, which is like a bird highway in the sky. Birds use these flyways to migrate between their summer and winter homes. Other monuments are home to birds that live there year-round.

This wordsearch contains the names of 15 birds you might spot in the national monuments. Can you find them all? The words might be written forward, backward, up, down, or diagonally.

OWL

CROSSBILL

RED-THROATED LOON

WOODPECKER

SWIFT

TURKEY VULTURE

HUMMINGBIRD

BALD EAGLE

SWALLOW

SPRUCE GROUSE

SANDHILL CRANE

ALBATROSS

PEREGRINE FALCON

PUFFIN

Both tufted and horned puffins live at Aniakchak, Alaska. In the air, a puffin's wings can beat at a speedy 400 times a minute.

J	B	A	L	D	E	A	G	L	E	L	I	N	D	U	P	H	D	U	P
S	U	T	U	Q	M	K	Q	D	L	X	T	O	F	K	T	N	N	U	R
S	A	N	F	R	T	S	Q	I	R	F	T	O	Z	T	S	Q	P	W	E
S	S	N	U	Z	Z	C	B	N	I	I	Y	L	R	Q	U	C	A	C	M
O	H	L	D	N	G	S	E	W	S	O	G	D	W	O	L	L	A	W	S
R	I	U	R	H	S	M	S	O	X	R	E	E	N	L	L	O	Z	H	P
T	I	V	M	O	I	R	G	J	E	T	B	T	O	K	B	I	Y	M	R
A	F	W	R	M	G	L	O	W	H	K	U	A	F	E	Z	M	O	H	U
B	M	C	D	M	I	M	L	V	M	R	N	O	P	X	V	R	S	H	C
L	A	E	R	E	O	N	F	C	K	T	K	R	U	W	A	L	L	B	E
A	N	F	E	F	W	U	G	E	R	J	N	H	F	L	T	K	Y	J	G
K	R	D	I	D	B	M	Y	B	Q	A	H	T	F	Z	W	K	P	A	R
G	N	G	U	O	I	V	Z	K	I	H	N	D	I	G	F	O	S	Q	O
R	H	I	I	Q	U	P	W	W	V	R	Y	E	N	C	V	I	E	R	U
Y	C	O	L	L	D	P	B	U	F	Y	D	R	T	J	F	W	I	Z	S
R	U	F	T	O	S	S	I	M	L	G	X	H	S	S	T	D	S	X	E
Z	V	U	I	K	B	T	C	D	D	W	O	O	D	P	E	C	K	E	R
L	R	G	F	P	N	O	C	L	A	F	E	N	I	R	G	E	R	E	P
E	T	T	S	M	C	P	B	T	W	S	B	H	T	J	M	Q	D	C	M
H	M	Y	K	F	I	T	Y	D	D	X	P	H	A	A	M	Y	N	H	J

In the tallgrass prairie of Pipestone, Minnesota, you might hear the bubbly song of the bobolink. These birds travel around 12,000 miles every year as they migrate between North and South America.

BOBOLINK

UNDER THE SEA

The oceans hold some of the world's most fascinating creatures and incredible geology. In the Pacific Ocean, several marine national monuments shelter these important—and increasingly threatened—places and species.

Rose Atoll, the southernmost island of American Samoa, is home to delicate corals, giant clams, and hundreds of colorful fish species. Can you spot and circle **six** differences between these two pictures of this national monument?

MISSION TO MARIANA TRENCH

The plunging underwater landscape of Mariana Trench is home to bubbling vents, undersea volcanoes, and strange deep-sea creatures. The deepest spot of this dark and mysterious place is deeper than Mount Everest is tall!

Imagine you are a scientist exploring in your underwater vehicle, when you spot something unusual. It could be a strange new creature, an underwater city, or something else — it's up to you! Write a report of your trip and draw what you have seen in the space below.

_____

_____

_____

_____

_____

KA-BOOM!

Did you know that the U.S. has more volcanoes than almost any other country? Some of the nation's most dramatic landscapes have been shaped by volcanic activity. The monuments on this page preserve some of these special places.

Take a look at these multiple-choice questions. To answer them, you'll need a little general knowledge, plenty of common sense, and some clever guesswork! Circle your answers.

1 Aniakchak in Alaska is part of a chain of over 450 volcanoes that lies around the Pacific Ocean. What is this chain of volcanoes known as?

RING OF WATER

RING OF EARTH

RING OF FIRE

2 When Mount St. Helens, Washington, erupted in 1980, the huge explosion wiped out miles of forest. How many?

3 SQUARE MILES (THE SIZE OF LINCOLN PARK IN CHICAGO)

227 SQUARE MILES (THE SIZE OF CHICAGO)

58,000 SQUARE MILES (THE SIZE OF ILLINOIS)

3 In the Mount St. Helens eruption, ash spewed into the air twice as high as most airplanes fly. How high is that?

150 YARDS

15 MILES

150 MILES

4 The eruption at Mount St. Helens was triggered by a massive earthquake. What is the machine that measures earthquakes called?

THERMOMETER

QUAKOMETER

SEISMOGRAPH

5 Astronauts have trained for missions in the volcanic landscape of a monument in Idaho—which one?

MISTY FJORDS

MUIR WOODS

CRATERS OF THE MOON

6 At Mariana Trench, you'll find mud volcanoes and thermal vents burping out gases. Where is this remote underwater monument?

PACIFIC OCEAN

MEDITERRANEAN SEA

LAKE MICHIGAN

7 Devils Tower in Wyoming was formed by hot liquid rock that bubbled up beneath the Earth's surface. What is this liquid rock called?

PLASMA

MAGMA

MACARONI

8 At Lava Beds monument, California, you can visit lava tube caves formed thousands of years ago. What is the sport of exploring caves called?

ORIENTEERING

ORIGAMI

SPELUNKING

Bear Island

With about 1,600 brown bears, Admiralty Island monument in Alaska has one of the highest concentrations of brown bears in the world. At Pack Creek Bear Viewing Area, you might see bears gathering to feast on migrating salmon, as majestic bald eagles soar overhead.

This eagle, mom bear, and baby bear are all catching salmon for their dinner. Can you work out how many each one catches, using the information below? Write the totals under their pictures.

- Half of the fish swim away and escape.
- The eagle catches one more fish than the mom bear.
- The mom bear catches three more fish than the baby bear.

Awesome Americans

Imagine having a national monument named after you! All of the monuments on this page honor amazing people who have played an important part in the nation's history.

Can you crack the codes to reveal the names of the monuments?

1 Rearrange the letters of each word from back to front to reveal the name of a monument in Virginia where a U.S. president once lived.

EGROEG NOTGNIHSAW ECALPHTRIB

- -

2 Cross out every third letter to reveal the name of a monument in California that was the home of an important labor leader, who demanded better pay and safer jobs for farmworkers.

CÉTSAPR E. ACHEÁVIEZO

- - - - - - - · - - - - - - -

3 Cross out each W, X, and Z to discover the name of a Mississippi monument that was the home of two important civil rights leaders.

XMEDGAXR WAXND MYXRLIWE ZEVEXRS HWZOME

- -

4 Replace each of these letters with the letter that comes immediately before it in the alphabet to reveal the name of a monument in Ohio that honors the first African American superintendent of a national park. (Write out the alphabet to help you!)

DIBSMFT ZPVOH CVGGBMP TPMEJFST

- -

The National Monument of You

Maybe, one day, your childhood home will become a national monument to YOU! Imagine people traveling for miles to visit the building where you grew up and to learn about your incredible life.

Let's fast-forward to the future and create a National Monument of You.

Name of monument: _____

State: _____

Why have you been honored with a national monument? Maybe you have worked to make the world a better place, invented or discovered something incredible, become the president—or all three! Write about your achievements here.

_____

_____

_____

Draw a picture of your home in the space below.

PLANT PAIRS

Take a look at all these beautiful flowers that grow in the national monuments. Only two of each flower are identical. Can you find and circle the matching pairs?

LADY SLIPPER ORCHIDS, found at Katahdin Woods and Waters monument in Maine, look like tiny shoes!

PRAIRIE CLOVER grows in Pipestone, Minnesota. Indigenous people use the flower as medicine.

The flowers of **AMERICAN PASQUE** are one of the first signs of spring at Jewel Cave monument.

Prickly **HEDGEHOG CACTI** grow at Montezuma Castle monument in Arizona. Watch where you sit!

DINO DIG

At Dinosaur National Monument, in Colorado and Utah, you can check out bones from *Stegosaurus*, the giant *Apatosaurus*, and the awesome *Allosaurus*. Paleontologists (scientists who study fossils) are still finding new dinosaur remains today.

Can you help this paleontologist discover some new dinosaur bones? The clues below will tell you which blank square she needs to start digging in. Cross out the squares as you eliminate them, then draw a bone on the one empty square that remains.

CLUES:

1. The bones are not in any of the squares surrounding (above, below, left, right, or diagonal) the Quarry Exhibit Hall.
2. They ARE in a square surrounding a dinosaur footprint.
3. They are not in a square immediately above or below a prairie dog burrow.
4. They are not in the same column or row as an ancient rock drawing.

ALIVE OR EXTINCT?

At the John Day Fossil Beds monument, in Oregon, scientists have found fossils from animals that lived 44 million years ago. Three of the animals on this page once roamed the John Bay Basin but are now extinct (no longer exist), while the others still live in the U.S. today. Can you guess which animals are extinct?

Read the information about each animal, then circle your answers.

1
This cave-dwelling animal breathes oxygen through its skin.
ALIVE | EXTINCT

2
This three-toed horse is tiny — about the size of a border collie dog.
ALIVE | EXTINCT

3
This deep-sea creature has fins that look like elephant ears, which it flaps to get around.
ALIVE | EXTINCT

4
This tiny animal weighs less than a medium-sized apple, but can bound 9 feet into the air.
ALIVE | EXTINCT

5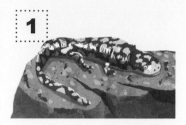
This lemur-like animal lives in the forests of Oregon and eats fruit.
ALIVE | EXTINCT

6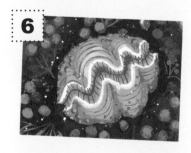
This underwater animal has special cells that use sunlight to make energy — just like a plant.
ALIVE | EXTINCT

7
This rabbit-like animal has fur on the soles of its feet and a loud squeak.
ALIVE | EXTINCT

8
This glow-in-the-dark creature lives 2 miles under the ocean's surface.
ALIVE | EXTINCT

9
This big, pig-like beast has bone-crushing jaws and is known as the "teminator pig."
ALIVE | EXTINCT

A New Discovery

Imagine you have discovered the first-ever fossil of a strange new animal that lived millions of years ago. What might it have looked like? Was it covered in feathers or fur? Maybe it was scaly or dripping with slime!

Give your discovery a name, describe it, and draw it in the space below.

Name: ....

National monument where it was discovered: ....
(You can choose an existing monument, or make up a new one.)

Where does it live? ....
(Underground? In the trees? In the ocean?)

What size is it? ....
(As big as a house? As small as a grain of rice?)

What does it eat? ....
(Plants? Other animals?)

FANTASTIC FORTS

The monumental forts along the East Coast are an American version of castles—some even have drawbridges and moats. Each fort provides a glimpse into the history of conflicts that have shaped this land.

Unscramble the anagrams below to find out which state each of these forts can be found in, then draw a line to match each one to the correct state outline. You can use the map at the front of the book to help you identify the shapes of the states.

FORT MONROE
This fort was a powerful Union stronghold during the Civil War.
GINVIRIA

1

CASTILLO DE SAN MARCOS
Dating from 1672, this is the oldest stone fort in the continental U.S.
LORFIDA

2
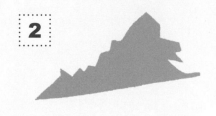

FORT STANWIX
This fort was built in 1758 on an important trading route.
WEN KORY

3

FORT McHENRY
The original "Star-Spangled Banner" flew here in the War of 1812.
MALANDRY

4

FORT PULUSKI
During the Civil War, soldiers played baseball here to pass the time!
GIAGEOR

5

Jewel Cave Maze

Sparkling crystals shine like buried treasure in Jewel Cave, in South Dakota. At more than 210 miles long, it's the third-longest cave in the world. There are many parts that still haven't been explored.

On a tour around the cave, this boy has become separated from the guide. Now he's hopelessly lost! Can you help him find his way out? Good luck!

EXIT

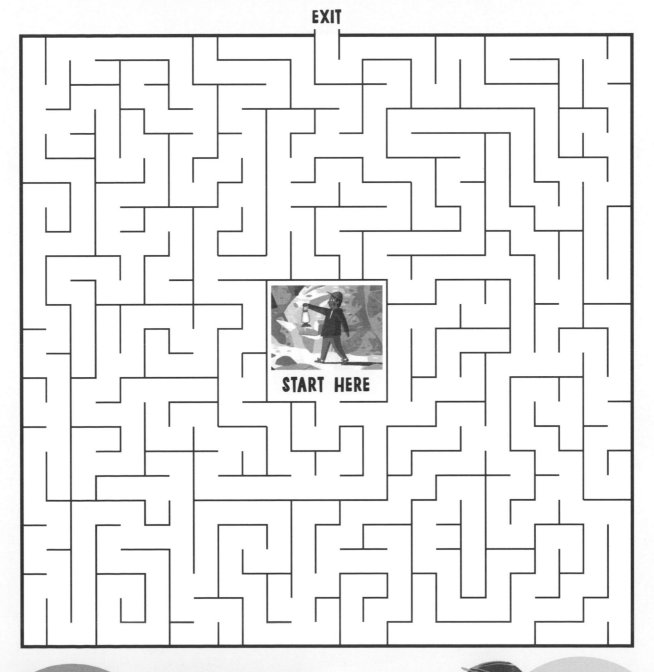

START HERE

Cave formations formed by dripping water are called speleothems.

Hundreds of Townsend's big-eared bats hibernate at Jewel Cave. When they're not flying, these bats sometimes curl their ears up like cinnamon rolls!

RACE ACROSS THE U.S.A.

It's time to take a final trip around the national monuments of the U.S.A. Along the way, you'll pass smoking volcanoes, historic houses, rushing rivers, and underwater wonderlands teeming with colorful fish.

To play this game, you'll need another player, a die, and two game pieces — these can be anything small, like coins or buttons. Take turns to roll the die and move your game pieces, following any instructions on the circle you land on. The winner is the first person to visit six different monuments AND reach the finish line.

START!

ROLL THE DIE TO BEGIN.

Explore the ancient cliff dwellings at **Bandelier** monument. Phew, you need a break after climbing all those ladders!

MISS A GO

At **Aniakchak**, raft a wild river from a volcanic crater lake to the ocean.

ROLL THE DIE: IF YOU ROLL 1-3, SHOOT FORWARD 3 SPACES. IF YOU ROLL 4-6, YOU CAPSIZE—DRIFT BACK 2 SPACES.

Stop to recharge at **President Lincoln and Soldiers' Home**, the former president's summertime retreat.

MISS A GO.

A lightning storm has hit the Verde Valley at **Montezuma Castle** monument. Take shelter until it passes.

MISS A GO

Uh-oh, **Mount St. Helens** is starting to rumble . . .

RUN BACK TO THE START— QUICKLY!

The mosquitos in the vast wilderness of **Misty Fjords** monument are big, and they're everywhere!
RUN BACK 2 SPACES

Lie back and gaze at the stars at **Cedar Breaks** monument, an International Dark Sky Park. Uh-oh, you've fallen asleep…
MISS A GO

Snorkel from reef to reef at **Pacific Remote Islands**.
SWIM FORWARD 1 SPACE

Take a wrong turn in the twisting passageways of **Oregon Caves**.
GO BACK 1 SPACE

Cruise along Rim Rock Drive in **Colorado monument** — one of the most beautiful drives in the West.
MOTOR FORWARD 1 SPACE

Peer up at giant redwood trees on a walk through **Muir Woods**.
STROLL FORWARD 1 SPACE

CONGRATULATIONS!

You've completed your trip! Have you visited six national monuments? If not, go back to the start and keep counting.

LETTER TO THE PRESIDENT

Today, there are around 130 national monuments in the U.S.A. But new monuments are created all the time. Some monuments are created by Congress, and others are created by the president.

Do you have a special spot in your neighborhood that you want to take care of? Maybe it's a favorite tree, a site for local wildlife, or a building where someone you care about lives.

Write a letter to the president to tell them why this special place should become the nation's newest national monument.

When you're finished, why not copy out your letter and send it to the White House for real?

Draw a picture of your special place here, or stick in photographs and other pictures to make a collage.

ANSWERS

Pages 2-3: Welcome!
Devils Tower-Wyoming
Papahānaumokuākea-Hawaii
Statue of Liberty-New York and New Jersey
Aniakchak-Alaska
Avi Kwa Ame-Nevada
George Washington Carver-Missouri

Page 4: Statue of Liberty in Numbers
Pennies-2
Rays in crown-7
Index finger-8
Steps-377
Immigrants-12 million
Birthday-100

Page 5: How Big?
659

Page 6: Study the scene
1. Two
2. Binoculars
3. Helicopter
4. Right
5. Bird (gull)
6. Two

Page 7: March for Equality
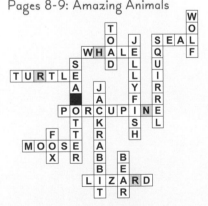

Pages 8-9: Amazing Animals

Fastest animal: pronghorn.

Pages 10-11: The First Americans
Pipestone-Minnesota
Montezuma Castle-Arizona
Rainbow Bridge-Utah
Devils Tower-Wyoming
Admiralty Island-Alaska
Papahānaumokuākea-Hawaii

Page 12: Thrill-seekers
Laila-sea kayaking-Misty Fjords
Adam-whitewater rafting-Dinosaur
Omar-cross-country skiing-Katahdin Woods and Waters

Page 13: Small and Beautiful
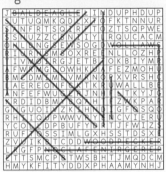

Pages 14-15: Bird Search
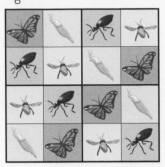

Page 16: Under the Sea

Page 18: KA-BOOM!
1. Ring of Fire
2. 227 square miles
3. 15 miles
4. Seismograph
5. Craters of the Moon
6. Pacific Ocean
7. Magma
8. Spelunking

Page 19: Bear Island
Eagle: five fish
Mom bear: four fish
Baby bear: one fish

Page 20: Awesome Americans
1. George Washington Birthplace
2. César E. Chávez
3. Medgar and Myrlie Evers Home
4. Charles Young Buffalo Soldiers

Page 22: Plant Pairs

Page 23: Dino Dig
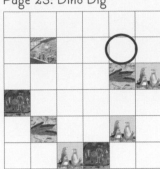

Page 24: Alive or Extinct?
1. Tiger salamander-ALIVE
2. *Orohippus major*-EXTINCT
3. Dumbo octopus-ALIVE
4. Kangaroo rat-ALIVE
5. *Ekgmowechashala zancanellai*-EXTINCT
6. Giant clam-ALIVE
7. Pika-ALIVE
8. *Crossota* jellyfish-ALIVE
9. *Archaeotherium caninus*-EXTINCT

Page 26: Fantastic Forts
Fort Monroe-Virginia-2
Castillo de San Marcos-Florida-3
Fort Stanwix-New York-1
Fort McHenry-Maryland-5
Fort Puluski-Georgia-4

Page 27: Jewel Cave Maze
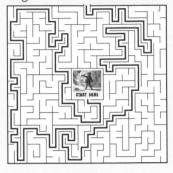

National Monuments of the U.S.A. Activity Book © 2024 Quarto Publishing plc.
Text © 2024 Quarto Publishing plc. Illustrations © 2023 Chris Turnham.
Based on National Monuments of the U.S.A. by Cameron Walker and Chris Turnham.

First published in 2024 by Wide Eyed Editions, an imprint of The Quarto Group.
100 Cummings Center, Suite 265D, Beverly, MA 01915, USA.
T +1 978-282-9590 F +1 078-283-2742 www.Quarto.com

A CIP record for this book is available from the Library of Congress.

ISBN 978-0-7112-8774-7
The illustrations were created digitally.
Set in Pistacho and School Hand

Written and edited by Claire Saunders
Published by Debbie Foy and Georgia Amson-Bradshaw
Designed by Lyli Feng
Production by Beth Sweeney

Manufactured in Guangzhou, China EB112023
9 8 7 6 5 4 3 2 1

FSC MIX Paper from responsible sources FSC® C124385